MW00399680

For

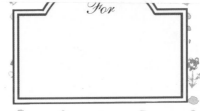

gift of
friendship

Written and compiled by Conover Swofford

Illustrated by Patsy Pennington

Designed by Arlene Greco

INSPIRE

Inspire Books is an imprint of Peter Pauper Press, Inc.

Text copyright © 1999
Peter Pauper Press, Inc.
202 Mamaroneck Avenue
White Plains, NY 10601
Illustrations copyright © 1998
Patsy Pennington, licensed by
Wild Apple Licensing
All rights reserved
ISBN 0-88088-122-4
Printed in China
7 6 5 4 3 2 1

Gift of friendship

Every good and perfect gift
is from God.

JAMES 1:17 (NIRV)

Nothing but heaven itself
is better than a friend
who is really a friend.

PLAUTUS

Friends love at all times.
They are there to help
when trouble comes.

PROVERBS 17:17 (NIrV)

Friendship, gift of Heaven,
delight of great souls.

VOLTAIRE

Two people are better than one. They can help each other in everything they do.

ECCLESIASTES 4:9 (NIrV)

After the friendship of God,
a friend's affection is the
greatest treasure here below.

ANONYMOUS

What is a friend?
A single soul dwelling
in two bodies.

ARISTOTLE

A faithful friend
is a secure shelter;
whoever finds one has
found a treasure.

ECCLESIASTICUS 6:14 (NEB)

You're terrific.
I hope you know
Our friendship will
Just grow and grow.

We're friends not only
because of what we have
in common but because
our differences complement
each other.

Carry each other's heavy
loads. If you do,
you will give the law of
Christ its full meaning.

GALATIANS 6:2 (NIRV)

[A] friend is the
hope of the heart.

RALPH WALDO EMERSON

There are three friendships
which are advantageous:
friendship with the upright,
with the sincere, and
with the man of
much observation.

A faithful friend
is beyond price;
his worth is more
than money can buy.

ECCLESIASTICUS 6:15 (NEB)

There are no debts
between true friends.

The love of a friend
is the most powerful
love on earth.

[T]he place you have in
[my] heart is such that,
come death, come life,
we meet it together.

2 Corinthians 7:3 (NEB)

The only way to have a
friend is to be one.

RALPH WALDO EMERSON

Definition of a friend:
Someone you can trust
with your secrets; who
will stand by you no
matter what; who always
loves and accepts you.

A true friend is the
gift of God, and he
only who made hearts
can unite them.

ROBERT SOUTH

God gave us the gift
of friendship so we could
know His love on earth.

A faithful friend is
an elixir of life,
found only by those
who fear the Lord.

ECCLESIASTICUS 6:16 (NEB)

I know I've never told you
In the hurried rush of days
How much your
friendship helps me
In a thousand little ways;
But you've played such a part
In all I try to be
I want to tell you thank you
For being friends with me.

Most of all,
love one another deeply.
Love erases many sins
by forgiving them.

1 PETER 4:8 (NIrV)

Life has no blessing
like a prudent friend.

EURIPIDES

I'm proud to
call you friend.

You have filled my heart
with great joy.

PSALMS 4:7 (NIrV)

He gained from Heav'n
('twas all he wished)
a friend.

THOMAS GRAY

Where you go I'll go.
Where you stay I'll stay.
Your people will be my
people. Your God will
be my God.

RUTH 1:16 (NIrV)

God gave you to me.

God gave you to me.

I'm as happy as can be!

God gave you to me.

Friendship uses our
troubles to bond
our souls together.

The man who fears the Lord keeps his friendships in repair, for he treats his neighbor as himself.

ECCLESIASTICUS 6:17 (NEB)

The only true friend
is an unselfish friend.

Don't hold back good
from those who are worthy
of it. Don't hold it back
when you can help.

PROVERBS 3:27 (NIrV)

A friend is someone
who shares your ideas
as well as your
conversations.

When God first thought
of me, I know He also
thought of you because
He knew I needed a friend.

I thank my God
every time
I remember you.

PHILIPPIANS 1:3 (NIrV)

Your friendship is
an even better gift than
birthday presents!

The best mirror
is an old friend.

GEORGE HERBERT

A friend never says
anything behind your
back that she wouldn't
say to your face.

Walk beside me, my friend,
down life's road so that
I can reach out and take
your hand when I need
a hand to hold.

. . . I have not stopped
thanking God for you.
I always remember you
in my prayers.

EPHESIANS 1:16 (NIrV)

In the Bible there were
David and Jonathan;
in Greek mythology,
Damon and Pythias;
on TV, Lucy and Ethel;
today, me and you.

I talked to God about
you today, but I didn't
mention you-know-what
because that's the kind
of friend I am.

A friend listens to
your heart and not
just your words.

Everyone should be quick
to listen. But they should
be slow to speak.

JAMES 1:19 (NIrV)

I know you are my friend
because together we
walk closer to God.

Friends believe in your
visions and encourage you
to follow your dreams.

God pours His love

through you to me.

We love because
He loved us first.

1 John 4:19 (NIrV)

A friend who stands
by you through any
circumstance no matter
what—that is a friend!

I will not be afraid to
protect my friend
nor will I turn my
back on him.

ECCLESIASTICUS 22:25 (NEB)

In this dark world
of gloom, you are
my ray of hope.

Wounds from a friend can be trusted. But an enemy kisses you many times.

Proverbs 27:6 (NIrV)

A friend loves
you enough to tell
you the truth.

A friend knows when your
business is her business
and when it is not.

Friendship survives
any distance.
(So you can run,
but you can't hide!)

A friend is a person
with whom I may be
sincere. Before him,
I may think aloud.

RALPH WALDO EMERSON

As iron sharpens iron,

so one person

sharpens another.

Proverbs 27:17 (NIrV)

When our minds
get together, sparks fly.

Those who erase a sin
by forgiving it show love.
But those who talk
about it come between
close friends.

PROVERBS 17:9 (NIrV)

Friends know you so well,
they don't even ask if a
rumor is true.

When a friend hears gossip
about you, she doesn't
repeat it.

May the Lord bless you and
take good care of you.

NUMBERS 6:24 (NIrV)

May the Lord smile
upon you and be
gracious to you.

NUMBERS 6:25 (NIrV)

May the Lord look
on you with favor and
give you His peace.

NUMBERS 6:26 (NIrV)

Of all the blessings
God has given me,
I thank Him most
for you.

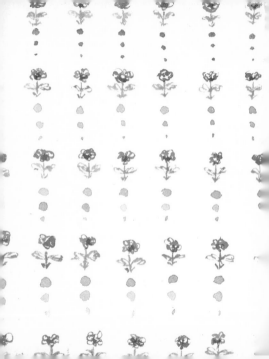